Selected Duets

for FRENCH HORN

Published in Two Volumes:

VOLUME I (Easy-Medium)

VOLUME II (Advanced)

Compiled and Edited

by **H. VOXMAN**

RUBANK®

HAL•LEONARD®
CORPORATION

7777 W. BLUEMOUND RD. P.O. BOX 13819 MILWAUKEE, WI 53213

PREFACE

Duet playing affords the student the most intimate form of ensemble experience. The problems of technique, tone quality, intonation, and ensemble balance are brought into sharpest relief. Careful attention must be given to style as indicated by the printed page and as demanded by the intangibles of good taste.

A number of the duets date from the eighteenth century and present problems in the interpretation of ornaments. In general, trills written before the year 1800, and probably many written thereafter, should begin with the note above the principal note.

The author wishes to express his thanks to the Trustees of the British Museum for permission to use materials obtained from that library.

H. Voxman

●

CONTENTS

●

Four Duets

Selected from the Works of Mozart

MOZART

MOZART

Menuetto

Three Canons
by James Winter

WINTER

BASED ON THE SCALE

WINTER

Allegretto grazioso

To be played entirely on the natural F Horn, without "correcting" the B♭ and F.

Non troppo allegro

WINTER

Nine Duets

Selected from the Works of Telemann, Monteclair, and Others

FANFARE

NAUDOT

Allegretto

18th Century

3

GAVOTTE

CORELLI

Dolce

TELEMANN

Largo (in three)

FUGUE

The **+** is a symbol for a short trill.

MONTECLAIR

Duo No. 1
by Kopprasch

Seven Duets

Selected from the Works of Corrette, Gallay,
Weller, Stamitz, and Jacqmin

PREMIER DIVERTISSEMENT

CORRETTE

★ The + is the symbol for a trill beginning with the upper auxiliary.

TAMBOURIN

GALLAY

Allegretto

GALLAY

Allegretto molto

FUGATO

STAMITZ

Minuetto vivace

Fine

TRIO Louré (legato)

Allegro moderato [in four]

JACQMIN

Four Duos

Selected from the Works of Vecchietti

VECCHIETTI

Allegretto

Tempo I

Allegro moderato (♩ = 112)

Allegro moderato (♩ = 132)

Nine Duos

Selected from the Works of Bach, Handel, Mozart, Franz, and Others

BIMBONI

MINUET

HANDEL

Un poco Larghetto

EXCERPT from the "WATER MUSIC"

HANDEL

Allegro

MOZART - TÜRRSCHMIEDT

SCHERZO

FRANZ

TRIO

Meno mosso

INVENTION XV

BACH-FRANZ

Andante

BACH-FRANZ

Allegretto

INVENTION III

BACH-FRANZ

INVENTION VIII

BACH-FRANZ

Moderato